CW01082736

Original Title: Veils of the Past

Editors: Theodor Taimla
Autor: Jessy Jänes
ISBN 978-9916-748-94-7

Veils of the Past

Jessy Jänes

Blanket of Antiquated Echoes

In cryptic whispers, shadows dance,
Through corridors of time's embrace,
Ancient stories take a stance,
Lost within the silent space.

Worn out pages, voices slight,
A chorus from the ages calls,
In twilight's soft, forgiving light,
We hear the past within the walls.

In echoes soft, we find our key,
To mysteries unsolved, unspoken,
Threads of yesterday weave free,
In hearts where time's spell is unbroken.

Ghostly fingers trace the lines,
Written on the winds of lore,
Each whisper's truth, a sign,
Of tales from epochs gone before.

Layered in the quiet night,
A tapestry of times foregone,
Blanket of echoes wrapped tight,
Lighting paths to worlds long drawn.

History's Veiled Path

Step by step, on cobbled roads,
Shrouded in a mist of grey,
Guarded tales from long ago,
Whisper what the stones relay.

Time-hued walls and mossy edges,
Keep the secrets dusk adorned,
On the brink of silent ledges,
Echoes of the past are born.

Through the mist, a shadow's form,
Merging with the sun's brief stay,
Stories lived through skies once stormed,
Carved on paths where spirits stray.

Feet that tread on history's cloak,
Feel the pulse beneath the grime,
Every stone and rooted oak,
Marks the journey of olden time.

In the veiled path's soft embrace,
Hidden from the watch of day,
We find the past's hushed, secret place,
In the whisper of paths astray.

Murmurs of Forgotten Eras

In shadows cast by ancient light,
Whispers drift through endless night,
Silent tales of bygone days,
Lost in time's elusive haze.

Ghosts of yesteryears remain,
Echoes bound by aching chains,
Yearning voices, soft and low,
Tales they speak, yet none shall know.

Songs of past, in wind they weave,
Murmurs only hearts believe,
Carried far on zephyrs' breath,
Through the valleys, over death.

Ancient Whispers in the Wind

Wind that howls through hollowed trees,
Sings of distant memories,
Ancient whispers, faint and clear,
Bringing past and present near.

Tales of kingdoms, long decayed,
Fortresses in ruins laid,
Heroes' names, in legends told,
Echo still, through forests old.

Soft as sighs of summer rain,
Comes the wind, with sweet refrain,
Binding thoughts of old and new,
In a murmur, deep and true.

Shrouds of Time Layers

Shrouds of time, like misty veil,
Cover secrets, old and frail,
Layered deep, beneath the night,
Hidden far from mortal sight.

Aged in whispers, shadows dance,
Through the corridors of chance,
Moments lost in sands that fall,
Time that governs, ones and all.

Glimpses of a world undone,
Fleeting as the setting sun,
In the depths of memory twined,
Shrouds of time, forever bind.

The Muffled Beat of Yore

In the depths of ages past,
Echoes of the first storm's blast,
Muffled beats of yore remain,
Haunting like a ghostly chain.

Every pulse of time long gone,
Resonates where shadows spawn,
Through the eons, soft and sure,
Heartbeats of an age impure.

Echoes linger, soft and deep,
In the silence secrets keep,
Muffled in their ancient lore,
Legends from the times before.

Sepia Mirages

Beneath the amber skies,
phantoms softly tread,
sand dunes whisper tales
of deserts long since dead.

Oases bloom with mirages
where lost dreams reside,
in sepia tones they linger,
on the canvas wide.

Footprints fade in twilight,
erasing all but sighs,
the sun dips in silence,
as the old world lies.

Nomads of forgotten time
retrace the past anew,
sepia shadows dance,
in the evening's hue.

Whispers fade to echoes
of a distant, bygone land,
sepia mirages shimmer,
golden grains of sand.

Remains of Another Era

Ancient stones long weathered,
ere's whispers from the past,
tell tales of lives once spoken,
in voices unsurpassed.

Forgotten empires crumble,
leave ruination's mark,
remains of another era,
in silence, still and stark.

Once grand halls, now shadows,
echoes fade, light dims,
we traverse through memories,
of once celestial hymns.

Ruins hum a sorrow,
sing a tune forlorn,
past glories lie entombed,
in the misty morn.

Time's slow dance surrounds us,
as histories converge,
the remains of yesteryears
in endless dreams emerge.

Ghostly Reflections

In the mirror's twilight sheen,
phantoms glimpse and wane,
ghostly reflections linger,
stitched by memory's chain.

Ephemeral apparitions,
caught in argent light,
whisper sacred secrets
only shared at night.

Visages of yore appear
beyond the silver glass,
specters of the long-lost,
flickering as they pass.

Silent echoes murmur,
tales from distant days,
haunting tender moments,
suspended in a haze.

Unveiled in subtle glimmers,
they weave a spectral lore,
ghostly reflections hover
where dreams and shadows soar.

Muffled Voices

Through the ancient hallways,
muffled voices creep,
from times ripe with stories,
woven in the deep.

Muted whispers travel,
through twilight's thickened air,
carrying lost fragments,
of moments rarest rare.

Subdued conversations,
echo in the dusk,
stealthy as the wind's breath,
soft and unhurried husk.

In the stillness lingered,
secrets softly tread,
muffled voices murmur,
tales of what is dead.

Among the shadows' cradle,
they find their quiet home,
muffled voices whisper,
forever they will roam.

Secrets Locked in Time's Keep

Whispers carved in ancient stone,
Echoes of a world unseen.
Stories of the lost, unknown,
Locked within a timeless dream.

Thrones of kingdoms, dust and gold,
Legends that the stars could tell.
Pages past that won't unfold,
Hidden where the shadows dwell.

Memories of moonlit nights,
Prayers of hearts turned cold and still.
Phantoms in forgotten lights,
Wandering in time's old mill.

Veils of history drawn deep,
Mysteries that silence swore.
In the night where shadows seep,
Time keeps secrets evermore.

The Concealed Yore

In the tapestries of dusk,
Woven tales of old remain.
Every thread a voice, a husk,
Whispering of joy and pain.

Ancient rivers 'neath the ground,
Flow with memories suppressed.
In the silence they are bound,
Secrets longing to confess.

Footsteps in deserted halls,
Echoes faint of laughter, cries.
Ghostly whispers through the walls,
'Midst the past that never dies.

Yet in dreams, the past is clear,
Shadows of the yore unfurled.
In the echoes, we can hear,
Silent songs of a lost world.

Draped in Bygone Mists

Morning mists that veil the past,
Over hills where legends sleep.
Dreams that in the shadows cast,
Tales the ancient mountains keep.

Shrouded paths of yesteryears,
Lead to realms of memory.
Through the veil of time and tears,
Sight beyond what eyes can see.

Silent specters guard the dawn,
'Neath the canopy of sky.
In their watch, the night withdrawn,
Secrets 'midst the whispers lie.

Veils of fog and twilight's glow,
Hide the truths of olden schemes.
In the depths where shadows grow,
Dwell the echoes of our dreams.

Time-Worn Shadows

Shadows dance in twilight's glow,
Figures from a time gone by.
Stories etched in ebb and flow,
Of a past that will not die.

Time-worn faces, time-worn lands,
Echoes of the days of old.
Silent songs from ancient sands,
Legends in the dark retold.

In the twilight, truths confide,
Whispers from the era's end.
Footprints where the phantoms hide,
Messages the shadows send.

Centuries in shadows lost,
Fables woven in the night.
Through the years and tempest's cost,
Time-worn shadows guard the light.

Hidden Echoes of Time

Whispers float on ancient winds,
Through corridors of forgotten lore.
Shadows dance where light rescinds,
Time's hidden echoes, forevermore.

Silent murmurs, long erased,
In the heart of history's folds.
Moments lost, unlived, ungraced,
Stories untold, memory holds.

Faint impressions on the air,
Echoes of a time begone.
Mysteries beyond compare,
Hidden truths in twilight drawn.

Cloistered Ancestries

In the cloisters of our past,
Echoes whisper of yore.
Ancient voices, shadows cast,
Whispers through time, implore.

Bloodlines twisted, stories spun,
Lives entwined, threads weave tight.
Ancestral paths, journeyed, run,
Through the veil of silent night.

In the silence, histories lurk,
Veiled by years, untold, unseen.
Buried deep, where secrets work,
In each cloistered ancestry screen.

Concealed Generations

Generations lost in mist,
Shrouded tales, unseen hands.
Life's short lives, quietly kissed,
By the passage through the sands.

Faces blurred, names erased,
From the annals of our lore.
Time's slow march, memories chased,
Into shadows, evermore.

Silent whispers of the past,
Speak of lives we never knew.
Concealed generations' cast,
Dreams forgotten, still pursue.

The Tapestry of Hidden Years

Threads of gold and silver spun,
In the tapestry of years.
Hidden lives, their courses run,
Woven with forgotten tears.

Echoes of a bygone age,
Stir in silence, softly flow.
Lines on history's quiet page,
Tell of times we'll never know.

Through the weft of days long gone,
Mysteries quietly appear.
In the fabric, dusk to dawn,
Lies the tapestry of hidden years.

Wrapped in Yesterday's Echo

In the quiet dusk where shadows play,
Whispers of the past softly sway,
Memories drift in the dying light,
Wrapped in yesterday's echo, away from sight.

Ghosts of dreams once held so tight,
Linger in the folds of night,
Glimmers of hope, though faint they glow,
Stories untold in the winds that blow.

The world moves on, yet time holds still,
Fragments of love on the window sill,
Through the haze, a distant call,
Wrapped in yesterday's echo, we'll recall.

Beneath Ancient Shrouds

In the cryptic depths where secrets lie,
Beneath ancient shrouds, the ages spy,
Wisps of legends in the forgotten tombs,
Silent echoes in the twilight glooms.

Veils of time, they gently fall,
Embracing tales that history enthralls,
Buried deep in the earth's embrace,
Are the whispers of an ancestral grace.

Shadows dance in the candle's glow,
Tracing patterns of long ago,
Echoes faint of love and plight,
Beneath ancient shrouds, they seek the light.

Flickers of Forgotten Light

In the somber shade where silence dwells,
Flickers of forgotten light cast spells,
Faintly glowing in the night,
Guiding us through shadows' flight.

Ephemeral glints of yesteryears,
Whisper stories through the tears,
Moments fleeting, yet they stay,
Flickers of light that guide our way.

Through the darkness, softly bright,
Hope emerges in the night,
In the heart, a spark ignites,
Flickers of forgotten light, we unite.

Through the Mists of Yesterday

Through the mists of yesterday we tread,
Seeking paths the ancients spread,
Footsteps echo in the dew-kissed morn,
Threads of fate so gently worn.

Lost in time yet never gone,
Memories like a timeless song,
Through the valleys, o'er the crest,
The heart's pilgrimage, never at rest.

Veiled in dreams of times gone by,
Underneath the ageless sky,
We walk, we pause, then fade away,
Through the mists of yesterday, we stay.

Phantom Hues

In the twilight of dreaming's shade,
Colors blend, then softly fade,
Phantom hues of dawn encroach,
In silence, they avidly encroach.

Whispers faint in midnight's fold,
Canvas dark, a story told,
Stars above begin to weave,
A tapestry of hope to believe.

Beneath the sky of velvet night,
Specters dance in soft moonlight,
Reflections kissed by whispered beams,
Cradle the softest of dreams.

On the edge of waking dawn,
Memories blink and then are gone,
Leaving shades of phantom hues,
In the morning's first soft muse.

The world reclaims its varied skin,
Another day will now begin,
Yet in my heart, those colors stay,
A phantom hue that guides my way.

Resonances of Yore

In chambers time has left behind,
Echoes of the bygone bind,
Resonances of yore resound,
In sepia tones they are found.

Voices lost in ages past,
In whispers swift, their shadows cast,
Haunting tunes of joys or woes,
Through the air in silence flow.

Ancient halls of memory's grace,
Each a story left to trace,
Laughter, tears, in chorus blend,
In the spaces memories send.

Olden songs in winds we hear,
Carry fragments on the ear,
Wisps of moments long revered,
Timeless, ageless, and endeared.

In the stillness of the night,
As stars adorn the ethereal light,
Resonances of the yore arise,
To meet the dawn with softened sighs.

Whispers of Yesteryears

In the corners of my mind's quiet eaves,
Whispers of yesteryears weave,
Tender murmurs of long-lost days,
In the dusky, fading rays.

Memories soft as morning dew,
Painted in a wistful hue,
Speak of times that came and flew,
Leaving shades in poignant view.

In echoes carried by the breeze,
With a touch of tender ease,
Lives and loves from days passed by,
Float like whispers through the sky.

In the glow of twilight's gleam,
Lingering in a wistful dream,
Yearning seems to softly sigh,
In the whispers that drift by.

Silent is the gentle call,
Of yesteryears that softly fall,
A symphony of times once near,
In the heart's most tender sphere.

Shadows of Forgotten Days

In the dim and distant haze,
Lie shadows of forgotten days,
Fleeting forms in memory's sea,
That fade like whispers, quietly.

Longing lingers in the air,
For moments that were once so fair,
Shadows cast by time's cruel hand,
Drift like grains of desert sand.

Each step in fields of yesterday,
Echoes paths we used to stray,
Now but shadows in the fog,
Footprints lost in memory's bog.

Ghostly wonders, faintly bright,
Glimmer in the soft moonlight,
Once they wove a life's embrace,
Now they find a phantom place.

In the heart, a gentle ache,
For shadows that do softly wake,
Forgotten days in slumber lie,
Beneath the vast and wistful sky.

Under Time's Secret Seal

In the quiet of eternal hush,
Where secrets deep align,
Lies a story faint and flush,
Under time's opaque design.

Threads of yesterdays interweave,
In a cosmic, silent deal,
Memories the heart cannot leave,
Under time's secret seal.

Whispers call from ageless sand,
Eons meld and voices kneel,
Holding fast to fate's command,
Under time's concealed appeal.

Mirrors coax the hidden past,
Every wound time will heal,
In the shadows they will last,
Under time's elusive zeal.

In the quiet, still domain,
Mysteries the stars reveal,
Lost in moments they remain,
Under time's eternal seal.

Concealed Shadows of Yore

Beneath the moon's soft, tender glow,
A tale ancient winds restore,
Echoes from the past bestow,
Concealed shadows of yore.

Veils of mist obscure the sight,
Histories in silence soar,
Guardians of ancient night,
Concealed shadows of yore.

Love and loss in whispers blend,
Ghosts of twilight on the shore,
Eternal stories never end,
Concealed shadows of yore.

Specters dance in faded grace,
Timeless realms they explore,
Unseen shades in life's embrace,
Concealed shadows of yore.

In our dreams, they softly tread,
Footsteps through a hidden door,
Amongst the memories of the dead,
Concealed shadows of yore.

Enfolded Ancestries

In the cradles of the night,
Veins of history run deep,
Past and present intertwined tight,
Enfolded ancestries keep.

Songs of old within our veins,
Echoes in the silence steep,
Whispers from the ancient reigns,
Enfolded ancestries heap.

Roots that anchor souls unseen,
Where the winds of centuries sweep,
Bound by threads that intervene,
Enfolded ancestries leap.

Generations' lasting trace,
In the heart they gently creep,
In our dreams, their ageless grace,
Enfolded ancestries seep.

Through the years, their spirits rise,
In the shadows as we sleep,
Love and blood, their endless ties,
Enfolded ancestries reap.

Silhouettes of Ancient Times

By candlelight, in dim-lit rooms,
Whispered tales of old demise,
Figures dance in ghostly plumes,
Silhouettes of ancient times.

Silent watchers of the night,
Drifting on the wind's soft chimes,
Histories in fragile light,
Silhouettes of ancient times.

Shadows cast by fire's glow,
Hold the secrets in their rhymes,
Past and present, ebb and flow,
Silhouettes of ancient times.

Through the veil of history,
Echoes of forgotten crimes,
Haunted by their mystery,
Silhouettes of ancient times.

In the twilight's subtle grace,
Lives once lived in silent mimes,
Ever-present, they embrace,
Silhouettes of ancient times.

Mists of Memory

In the gentle mists of memory
Lies a field of endless green
Whispers of a time gone by
Where we've often been

Shadows dance upon the past
Faintly tracing stories old
Echoes of a tender laugh
In the twilight's golden fold

Faces form in cloudy haze
Smiling through the years long gone
Moments locked in time's embrace
Beneath the rising dawn

Silent songs the heart will keep
In the mists that softly fade
Dreams that live within our sleep
In the memories we've made

Though the years may drift apart
Mists of memory will remain
Treasures safe within the heart
Binding us like gentle rain

Reminders of Ages Past

Ancient trees and weathered stone
Echo songs of yesteryear
Whispers of a time once known
In each leaf and drop of tear

Castles rise in misty morn
Holding secrets long concealed
Remnants of a life well-worn
In their shadows now revealed

Arrows lodged in wooden beams
Tales of battles fought and lost
Haunt the silence with their screams
Echoes of the fearless cost

Weathered books with pages worn
Hold the wisdom, shadows vast
Stories of a world reborn
Reminders of ages past

In the starlight and the breeze
Ancient whispers hold us fast
Binding us with memories
Reminders of ages past

Echoed Footsteps

In the quiet, echoed footsteps
Hold the song of days gone by
Ghostly in their soft procession
Underneath a twilight sky

Worn trails speak of journeys taken
Paths that wind through ancient trees
Steps of those who came before us
Drifting on the evening breeze

Echoed steps on cobbled streets
Mark the lives that once did pass
Leave impressions in the silence
Mirrored in the broken glass

Softly tread the echoed footsteps
Bearing tales of loss and love
Marking time in sacred rhythm
Guided by the stars above

In their dance we find reflections
Of the souls who walked this way
Echoed footsteps hold connections
Binding past to present day

Recollections of Yesteryears

Recollections of yesteryears
Paint a canvas wet with tears
Brushstrokes of a bygone day
Echo in the light's soft play

Laughter in the autumn breeze
Whispers through the ancient trees
Memories that softly call
Echo down the quiet hall

Children's games and joyful cries
Underneath the summer skies
Time has stored them in its chest
Moments of a life's sweet quest

Photos faded, edges worn
Hold the days of dreams reborn
Gentle smiles, a lover's glance
Captured in a fleeting dance

Recollections softly glow
In the heart, we always know
Presence of the yesteryears
Lingers in our joy and tears

Fading Portraits

In the attic, dust devours
Old frames filled with forgotten hours
Whispers of laughter, shades of tears
Echoes of life from bygone years

Brush strokes gentle, colors fade
Memories in silence laid
Once bright eyes now dimmed and gray
Time erases, night and day

Hidden stories in each glance
Of love, regret, a missed chance
In the attic, secrets keep
Portraits lost in quiet sleep

Canvas whispers, silent sigh
Underneath the silent sky
The past, a whispered serenade
In the shadows where they've stayed

Nostalgia's bittersweet embrace
Fading portraits, time's own trace
Eyes that saw, hearts that beat
Now left in the attic's retreat

Silent Chronicles

Pages worn with age and care
Tales forgotten linger there
In the silence, stories told
A voice from memories old

Ink that whispers through the years
Echoes of both joy and tears
Silent chronicles unfold
Mysteries in shadows hold

Every line a world within
Whispers of what might have been
Chapters lost to time's embrace
Linger in this quiet place

Beneath the dust, truth concealed
Life's lessons once revealed
Silent chronicles remain
Echoing loss, love, and pain

Worn pages, fragile hands
Time's own shifting sands
A glimpse into the past's keep
In silence, they gently sleep

Invisible Imprints

Steps that mark the sands of time
Invisible, yet so sublime
Footprints in the heart remain
Enduring through the joy and pain

Touch the wind, feel the trace
Invisible imprints leave their place
Moments shared in fleeting grace
Echoes in life's vast space

A smile, a word, a fleeting glance
Invisible threads of circumstance
Weaving through each day, each night
Leaving marks, though out of sight

Love's whisper, sorrow's cry
Leaving imprints as years go by
Invisible, yet always there
In every breath, in every prayer

Though unseen, they shape our days
Invisible imprints, life's own ways
In every memory, every dream
They flow like an endless stream

Phantoms of History

Echoes from the past arise
In shadows where the silence lies
Phantoms of history, quiet grace
Haunting every time-worn place

In ruins, whispers soft and low
Tales of worlds from long ago
Phantoms drifting through the night
Silent keepers of the light

Ancient walls and worn-out stone
Stories etched, yet almost gone
Phantom voices call in vain
From an era's distant plain

Histories in ghostly form
Hover through the quiet storm
Unseen, yet their presence near
Bringing past to present's sphere

Time's guardians silently stand
Phantoms of a lost command
History's breath, faint and wary
In each ghostly glance, they tarry

Timeworn Tales

In aged books of memories confined,
Lies the life that once was primed.
Pages yellowed, edges worn,
Stories told before we were born.

Whispers of yesterdays in the air,
Echoes of voices everywhere.
Olden dreams in sepia tones,
Etched in leather, ink, and bones.

Tales of love and warring skies,
Tales where heroes never die.
Fables weave through cobwebs gray,
Guiding us to a bygone day.

Each letter speaks of ancient lore,
Unraveling threads from years before.
Timeless words that never age,
In the silence, they still engage.

Ruffled pages, secrets deep,
In their embrace, memories sleep.
Timeworn tales forever stay,
Leading hearts a world away.

Buried Reminiscences

Beneath the surface, hidden away,
Lies the light of a former day.
Memories cherished, secrets sealed,
In hearts, the past is revealed.

Subtle whispers of the past,
In silent halls, shadows cast.
Buried deep where no eyes see,
Fragments of forgotten glee.

Locked in time, an old refrain,
Loss and love, joy and pain.
Resonating in distant dreams,
Echoes of long-lost themes.

Fields of gold and skies so blue,
Moments cherished, pure, and true.
In quiet corners they abide,
Soft reminders by our side.

Silent tales no longer told,
Treasured in the heart's stronghold.
Buried reminiscences unfold,
In memory, eternally bold.

Fallen Leaves of Time

Crimson paths where leaves descend,
Marking seasons, defining ends.
Whispers carried by the breeze,
Chronicles of time's decrees.

Moments draped in golden hues,
Fading branches, morning dews.
Nature's cycles subtly align,
In the fallen leaves of time.

Rustling secrets in the wind,
Time's embrace does gently mend.
Each leaf a story, softly fraught,
With memories time has wrought.

Autumn paints on nature's page,
A gallery of every age.
Leaves that drift, serene, sublime,
Fallen echoes of past prime.

Twilight shadows softly speak,
Time's frail canopy grows weak.
In the dusk, a calm divine,
Lies the fallen leaves of time.

Lost in Nostalgia's Gaze

In the heart where moments dwell,
Lies a wistful, tender spell.
Eyes that see through time's clear haze,
Lost in nostalgia's gentle gaze.

Sunsets glowing, soft and mild,
Memories of a playful child.
Dreams where faded laughter stays,
Held in nostalgia's warm embrace.

Echoes of a laughter's song,
Moments past where we belong.
Every smile, every phase,
Lost in nostalgia's gentle gaze.

Starlit nights and moonlit streams,
Glorious sights in memory's seams.
In the past where vision strays,
Lost in nostalgia's tender gaze.

Time moves on, yet hearts remain,
Bound by love, joy's sweet reign.
Remembered softly, day by days,
Lost in nostalgia's timeless gaze.

Cloaked in Forgotten Tales

Ancient books on dusty shelves
Whisper secrets time conceals
Tales of heroes, love, and wails
Shrouded by history's veils

In the library's quiet hush
Echoes of the past they brush
Words that once ignited fire
Silent now, yet still inspire

Scrolls of parchment, faded gold
Stories that were never told
Opuses of life and dreams
Hidden 'neath the moonlight's beams

Runes of wisdom etched in stone
Names that time has left alone
Legends of a world unseen
Embedded in the pages' sheen

Lost in time but not erased
Memories so gently placed
In the corners of our minds
Cloaked in tales, the past unwinds

Enshrouded Histories

Figures from forgotten lore
Silent on the temple floor
Whispers float like autumn leaves
Secrets that the night retrieves

Carved in walls of ancient tombs
Stories rise like morning blooms
Histories of gods and kings
Shrouded by time's endless rings

In the echoes, voices call
Footsteps fade along the hall
Chapters of a world concealed
By the hands of fate revealed

Myths and legends intertwined
Fragments of a grand design
Through the mists of time we see
Shadows of what used to be

Enshrouded histories unveil
Past's enigma, subtle trail
From the dark the truths emerge
Songs of time, forever surge

Shadows under Dust

Beneath the dust of ancient lies
Secrets of the past arise
Shadows cast by flickered light
Stories lost in endless night

Cobwebs draped on whispered truth
Hidden clues of age and youth
Buried deep within the husk
Mysteries of dawn and dusk

In the silence shadows creep
Guardians of dreams they keep
Fragments of a time once bright
Veiled in darkness, out of sight

Histories that time forgot
Traces of a secret plot
Words that once the heart enflamed
Covered now in ash unnamed

Through the darkened haze we peer
Eyes of minds that once were clear
Shadows dance beneath the crust
Echoes whisper under dust

Echoes behind the Curtain

Curtains drawn, the stage is bare
Echoes fill the silent air
Footprints left by those who tread
On the paths where dreams are spread

Faintly heard, the laughter's song
Memories of tales so strong
Ghostly visions flit and weave
Through the dreams they once conceived

Behind the curtain, shadows play
Whispers of another day
Voices of the unseen cast
Reveries from ages past

In the dim, the actors wait
For the turns of time and fate
Scenes that once were vivid, bright
Now just echoes in the night

Through the veils we glimpse the beams
Distant worlds and faded dreams
Curtains part, revealing then
Echoes of what might have been

Silent Tales of History

Whispers of ages long gone by
Echoes in ancient halls lie
Silent shadows cast their spell
In twilight where secrets dwell

Monuments stand in quiet grace
Guarding the past in solemn space
Forgotten voices blend in air
Ghostly murmurs everywhere

Granite walls, they softly weep
Memories in their silence keep
Cloaked in dusk, time's shadows cast
Dreams and tales of what's long past

Muffled sounds of steps once known
Through corridors where winds have blown
In the hush of night they speak
Of days once bright, now antique

History's breath on stone and clay
Whispers of what's gone away
A silent vigil, ever strong
Tells the tales where they belong

Hidden By Time's Haze

In a veil of misty grey
Lie stories of another day
Covered deep in morning's dew
Where time's hand remains askew

Forgotten fields and silent lands
Once held dreams within their hands
Echoes fade in the quiet air
Seeking solace ever there

Shadows drift on winds unseen
Of places where the world has been
Melodies of yesteryear
Softly hum for those who hear

Beneath the ancient, weathered trees
Rest the secrets borne on breeze
Time conceals what it bestows
In hidden paths that nature knows

Quietly the moments blend
A dance that seems to never end
In the haze, the past remains
Bound by unseen, timeless chains

Through Time's Drapery

Curtains drawn 'cross eras cold
Hiding mysteries untold
Through the folds of time's parade
Histories fade, then degrade

Glimpses spark in twilight's seam
Of a past that's like a dream
Moments faint, now memories
Caught within this temporal breeze

Ancient days slip through the veil
Ephemeral, like ships they sail
Stitched with threads of long gone lore
Drifting ever, yet no more

Tattered cloth of years gone past
Whispers truths that seldom last
Veiled in mists of woven time
Lost in rhythm, silent rhyme

Through drapery, the ages peer
Phantoms of what's once been near
Ever caught in spectral glow
In their silent, timeless flow

Ghosts of Old Stories

Echoes of the past arise
Wandering through the twilight skies
Ghosts of tales once told in light
Now they haunt the edge of night

Ancient myths and legends old
By the firelight were told
In the stillness, they remain
Whispers in the falling rain

Phantoms of lore roam the land
Invisible to the hand
Yet their presence lingers on
Long after the day has gone

Memories of tales once spun
Like shadows beneath the sun
Woven in the tapestry
Of lost time and mystery

Ghosts of old stories, they sigh
In the wind, they softly cry
Carrying tales of yore's delight
Through the veil of endless night

Traces of Ancestors

In the whispers of the pines,
Deep within the ancient loam,
Echoes of past, entwined,
Speak of hearth and distant home.

Carved stones whisper lore,
Of lives lived in twilight's grace,
Their footsteps through the door,
A silent, sacred place.

Moonlight on the weathered bark,
Stories etched in solemn tone,
Legacy in embers spark,
In hearts to call their own.

Old songs from lips straight line,
Passages through time they stream,
Carved in wind, the unseen sign,
History like a waking dream.

In the roots, their spirits swell,
Silent guardians of time,
In the stories, we dwell,
Searching past for hope's rhyme.

Lingering Memories

In the quiet of the dawn,
When shadows intermingle,
Whispers of what's gone,
Begin their haunting jingle.

Dusty frames on mantle high,
Hold lifetimes in their grasp,
Faces, names, that never die,
In lingering mem'ries clasp.

Beneath the willow's ancient arms,
Echoes softly breathe,
Moments held in time's charms,
In silence, souls do seethe.

Nightfall brings a gentle haze,
A dance of bygone eras,
In the twilight's tender gaze,
Love's ghostly cuentos.

Embrace the fading light,
Where memory gently flows,
In the heart's eternal fight,
The past forever glows.

Unraveled Histories

In the seams of time's old quilt,
Threads of stories lie,
Every patch a life that's built,
Underneath the sky.

Pages yellowed, letters fade,
Yet whispers still relay,
Of battles that were bravely made,
And nights turned into day.

Old maps with wrinkled lines,
Chart paths of heart and soul,
Voyages that span the pines,
To destinations whole.

Artifacts in shadows cast,
Tell tales of yesteryears,
Echoes in the present massed,
Dissolve away our fears.

In the weave of past we see,
Histories that intertwine,
Threads unraveled, yet they free,
The stories we define.

Elusive Shadows

Beneath the silver moon's soft glow,
Dancing shadows mar the plain,
Figures flicker, come and go,
Like whispers in the rain.

Silent as the wings of night,
They glide through memory's haze,
Markers of an ancient light,
Lost in time's deep maze.

Steps that echo, faint and low,
In corridors of dreams,
Spectres of what we don't know,
Flow through phantom streams.

Eyes that shimmer, unseen grace,
Phantoms of forgotten lore,
Glimmering in the empty space,
Where past and future pour.

Elusive as the morning mist,
They vanish in the day,
Eternal shadows, spirits kissed,
Forever fade away.

Echoes of Bygone Times

Beneath the canopy of whispering trees,
Ancient stories ride on the breeze.
Footsteps fade on forgotten paths,
Laughter lingers in the aftermath.

Shadows dance in the twilight's glow,
Whispering secrets only the old know.
Silent echoes of a world once bright,
Fading gently into the night.

Worn-out letters and sepia dreams,
Filling up the silken seams.
Time's gentle hand erases sorrow,
Promising a new tomorrow.

A distant song that still resounds,
In empty chapels, sacred grounds.
The present bows to yesteryears,
Honoring the lore of pioneers.

Amidst the ruins, joy entwines,
Everlasting, the echoes of bygone times.

Murmurs from Long Ago

In quiet chambers, where memories sleep,
Ancient voices softly weep.
Dreams from days of sun and rain,
Whisper secrets, pleasure, and pain.

Through cracked windows, breezes hum,
Songs from a world long succumbed.
Candles flicker with faint desires,
Sparking the heart's forgotten fires.

Old portraits on the dusty walls,
Silent witnesses to grand balls.
Echoes of laughter, joy that binds,
Murmurs from long ago, in kind.

Melodies of a thousand sighs,
Glimpses of forgotten skies.
Veils of time conceal the glow,
Yet through the silence, whispers flow.

Amongst the shadows, spirits surge,
Murmurs from the past, gentle and urgent.

The Faded Chronicles

Yellowed pages, tales untold,
Histories burnished, legends bold.
In each line, a voice revived,
Lives once lived, desires unbridled.

Ink-stained whispers shape the spine,
Of chronicles that stand divine.
Time's tender brush adds mystery,
To every faded memory.

Scrolls and scripts of ancient lore,
Locked behind a dusky door.
Characters of might and grace,
Inhabiting a vanished space.

Fragments of a world serene,
Held within a sepia screen.
Voices from the parchment rise,
Unfolding under curious eyes.

Lost in stories, hearts refine,
Treasures in these faded chronicles shine.

Memories Cloaked in Mist

In the shroud of early dawn,
Memories like ghosts are drawn.
Through the haze, old songs appear,
Echoes of a yesteryear.

Barefoot whispers on the sand,
Tracing steps of a distant land.
Misty veils of twilight's kiss,
Wrap around these moments' bliss.

Glimmers from a hidden past,
Fleeting as the shadows cast.
Thick with silence, thin with time,
Voices lost in fog's chime.

Soft reminders, gentle sighs,
In the realm where reverie lies.
Through the ether, dreams persist,
Memories cloaked in morning mist.

From dusk to dawn, they coexist,
Whispering through the veils of mist.

Curtains of Nostalgia

Through the muslin dreams we weave,
Faded colors, tales to grieve,
Whispers in the silent eaves,
Time's embrace, we gently cleave.

Memories hung like autumn leaves,
Softly brushing twilight sheaves,
Windows show what heart believes,
Life's old coat that time retrieves.

Echoes of the past arise,
Seen through those nostalgic eyes,
In the dance of dusk's disguise,
Long-forgotten lullabies.

Moonlit shadows softly pull,
Threads of yesteryears so full,
Gently, they begin to lull,
Stories weave their dreamy lull.

Curtains part, reveal the scenes,
Hidden dreams and silent means,
What has been or might have been,
Through the veil, we glimpse between.

Coverlet of Ancient Days

Wrap me in that ancient hue,
Threads of time in spectrums blue,
Every stitch, a story true,
Binding old and weaving new.

From the distant past it came,
Woven with a skill and flame,
Echoes whispering the same,
Tales engraved within its frame.

Softly draped in twilight's cast,
Every fold a spell to last,
Through its weave the shadows passed,
Memories from eras vast.

Soft embrace of yesteryears,
Calms the heart and soothes the fears,
Whispered dreams within the spheres,
Through the veil of time appears.

Coverlet with tales imbued,
Generations thus renewed,
In the fabric truths construed,
Ancient echoes once pursued.

Secrets Beneath the Dust

Beneath the dust, the secrets lie,
Unseen whispers, soft and dry,
History's voice, a gentle sigh,
In the shadows, truths deny.

Old books with pages turned to grey,
Hold the past from light of day,
Words unspoken, tales that stay,
Timeless echoes in delay.

Fragile whispers yearn to tell,
Locked in time's enduring cell,
Silent truths that once befell,
In the dust where secrets dwell.

Forgotten trinkets left behind,
Hints of stories, yet unlined,
Hidden realms within confined,
Veiled in time's relentless bind.

Through the mist of years accrued,
Lies the past, veiled and subdued,
Silent truths in dust ensued,
Timeless echoes still renewed.

Yesterday's Hidden Faces

Faces veiled by times gone by,
Hidden far from prying eye,
Memories in shadows fly,
Ghosts of yesteryears nearby.

Photographs of black and white,
Silent stares in faded light,
Glimpses of their silent plight,
Visages in ancient night.

Whispered names that life erased,
In the corridors of pace,
Lingering in silent grace,
Yearning for a brief embrace.

Echoes of their laughter stay,
In the whispers far away,
Silent actors in the play,
Lost to twilight and to day.

Faces of a time once new,
Seen by only but a few,
In the mist they hold the clue,
To the dreams they once pursued.

The Hidden Murmur

Beneath the leaves, a secret sighed,
In softest tones where shadows bide,
A murmur hushed, yet crystal clear,
Whispers only hearts can hear.

Among the trees with twilight's glow,
Mysteries in the night-time show,
A tale of days now lost in time,
Captured in a subtle rhyme.

The breeze it carries, tender, light,
Fragments of a distant sight,
Of love that never fades away,
In shadows where the spirits play.

Deep in the forest, guarded well,
Echoes of a hidden spell,
Hear the murmurs call you near,
To a world both strange and dear.

In twilight's grip, the secrets blend,
A murmured chant that has no end,
Unveiling what is left concealed,
In its quiet world revealed.

Drapes of Ancient Whispers

Veils that fall with evening's sigh,
Echoes draw where ghosts reside,
Speak of days in dusky hues,
Beneath the moon's reflective clues.

Old stones hold the tales of yore,
Curtains drift and shadows pour,
Whispers weave within the breeze,
Ancient voices among the trees.

Beneath those drapes so softly swung,
Songs of ages from lips unsung,
Tales of warriors, myths of love,
Carried by the wings above.

In twilight's shroud, the stories flow,
Like rivers of a timeless glow,
Each whisper threads the darkened night,
Drawing close the hidden light.

Wind will cast the drapes aside,
Revealing histories deep inside,
Listen close, the whispers hail,
In the ancient, timeless tale.

December Dreams of Yesteryear

In snowy fields where memories lie,
Ghosts of past December sigh,
Dreams of yesteryear unfold,
Stories of the nights so cold.

Candles flicker in the night,
Reflections of a gentle light,
Each flame recalls a distant cheer,
In dreams of frosty yesteryear.

Snowflakes drape the silent trees,
Songs of time on winter's breeze,
Carols sung in softest tones,
Resonate through icy bones.

The hearth recalls a warmth so dear,
Echoes from a bygone year,
Gathered close, the tales remain,
In the dreams that mark the lane.

Each December brings a thread,
Of golden memories long dead,
Yet alive in dreams we share,
Of yesteryears that still are fair.

Wrapped In Silent Lore

Folded in the arms of night,
Stories spin in soft moonlight,
Wrapped in lore of silent grace,
Memories in hidden place.

Books unopened, letters keen,
Silent whispers in between,
Pages turn with phantom hand,
Trails of worlds in twilight land.

Secrets whispered, wisdom old,
Wrapped in tales of legends bold,
Histories in quiet form,
Beneath the stars, they softly swarm.

Through the silence, voices trace,
Fables of another space,
Echos of a different shore,
In the silent lore they pour.

Veiled in night where stories dwell,
In the quiet, they compel,
Wrapped in silence, they endure,
Tales of life both clear and pure.

Curtains of the Unremembered

In the darkened quiet of the mind,
Unseen memories gently sweep.
Forgotten echoes left behind,
In twisted paths, they slowly creep.

Shadows cast on visions blurred,
Whispers lost in silent air.
Curtains fall without a word,
Of moments past beyond compare.

The veils conceal what once was bright,
Hidden stories left untold.
Curtains block the inner light,
Inward tales of ages old.

Grains of time in hidden strands,
Weave a fabric worn and thin.
Layers deep as shifting sands,
Cover what was held within.

In the folds of the unremembered,
Faded faces softly lie.
Curtains drawn, yet still dismembered,
Flights of time, unseen, pass by.

Epochs under Wraps

Epochs swathed in muted hues,
Silent ages wrapped in night.
Time encased in shadows' views,
Veiled from all but phantom sight.

Pages turned yet left unread,
Chronicles in hushed delay.
Histories by whispers led,
Bound in secrets gone astray.

Legends slumber under wrap,
Dreams entangled with each eve.
Myths that time's own hand does map,
Hidden deep, we must perceive.

Moments veiled by distant pasts,
Locked in silence, lost to grace.
Ages underneath amass,
Stories stored in careful trace.

Wrapped in epochs' subtle grip,
Tales concealed from present grasp.
Timeless clasps that never slip,
Holding history in their clasp.

Time's Subtle Drapery

Time unfurls its gentle folds,
Drapes of moments deftly sewn.
Each small thread a story holds,
Tales of lives and dreams unknown.

Softly flowing through the years,
Fabric woven from the past.
Seamless blend of joy and tears,
Memories that ever last.

Tapestry of life and love,
Subtle drapery so fine.
Weaving paths below, above,
Stitched within the grand design.

Every fold in time reveals,
Threads of gold and silken strands.
Lining where the truth unseals,
Shaping life with tender hands.

Underneath the subtle lies,
In the weave of time's embrace.
Hidden truths and quiet ties,
In the drapery of space.

Veiled Whispers of History

Whispers trace the silent years,
Histories veiled in the mist.
Softly speaking through our tears,
Shadows by the past now kissed.

Veiled in whispers subtle told,
Tales of yore in secrets laid.
Ancient echoes, songs of old,
Through the veils they softly wade.

Ghostly voices in the night,
Stories whispered, breaths of lore.
Shrouded in a hidden light,
Bygone days they're yearning for.

Histories cloaked in mystic veils,
Languages of time and place.
Softly told in winds and gales,
Pages left without a trace.

In the whispers of the past,
Veiled in shadows faintly drawn.
History's drapes are tightly fast,
Till the dawn reveals the yawn.

Relics of Quiet Hours

In the stillness of twilight's embrace,
Soft whispers dance through the air.
Shadows weave their tender lace,
Carving peace from the depths of despair.

Old books rest on timeworn shelves,
Pages yellowed by the hand of time.
Echoes of lives once led by themselves,
Resonate with an ancient chime.

Ceramic memories gather dust,
Silent sentinels of forgotten lore.
Each piece tells a tale of trust,
Of dreams that gently swam ashore.

Cobwebs cradle dreams of yore,
In frames where laughter used to gleam.
Relics of quiet hours explore,
Spaces where we dare to dream.

A clock ticks softly in the gloom,
Its hands tracing moments past.
In this quiet, sacred room,
Relics of time forever last.

Drapes of the Ancients

Heavy curtains drawn to seal,
The secrets of old, of life concealed.
Intricate patterns, they reveal,
Tales of worlds long forgotten, healed.

Woven threads of destiny,
Crossing paths in fabric's weave.
Stories spun in silent plea,
Of sorrow, love, and to believe.

Shadows shift in muted light,
Beneath the drapes, they softly play.
Ancient whispers in the night,
Guiding souls who've lost their way.

Each fold a vestige of the past,
In timeless dance they come alive.
Echoed whispers, shadows cast,
Where history and present thrive.

Through the drapes, the light shall pierce,
And paint the room with a golden hue.
From the ancients, messages fierce,
Transcending time, ever true.

Under Time's Shadow

Beneath the clock's unyielding gaze,
Moments slip like grains of sand.
We walk through life in a daze,
Guided by fate's gentle hand.

Time's shadow stretches long and deep,
Across the years we come to know.
In waking hours and in sleep,
Its silent whispers ebb and flow.

Memories etched in fading light,
Of days gone by, both near and far.
Under time's shadow, stars ignite,
Our inner compass, guiding star.

Each second a fleeting gift,
A chance to make our vision clear.
Under time's shadow, our spirits lift,
And forge ahead, devoid of fear.

Infinite moments, one by one,
Are strung together, true and slow.
Our legacy beneath the sun,
In time's embrace, forever flow.

Covered in Yesteryear's Gloom

Old photographs in black and white,
Capture moments lost to time.
Faded faces, out of sight,
Whisper tales in silent rhyme.

Cobwebs clung to memories,
Veiling dreams that once were bright.
Covered in yesteryear's demise,
A poignant relic of delight.

Broken toys and dusty shelves,
Remnants of a childhood past.
Silent echoes of ourselves,
Calling from a time held fast.

Relics draped in sorrow's shroud,
Haunt the corners of the room.
Whispering secrets, soft yet loud,
Smothered in yesteryear's gloom.

Yet through the sadness, hope does bloom,
In the shadows of forgotten years.
From yesteryear's encasing gloom,
We rise, triumphant over fears.

Stories Hidden in Time

Beneath the sands, where secrets lie
Whispers of epochs softly sigh
Ancient echoes call to mind
Tales in shadows left behind

In carved stone, the past breathes deep
Memories in quiet, endless sleep
Lost tales of love, of wars won and fought
By time, they're never once forgot

Leaves of yesteryears rustle and twine
Through ages, they dance, intertwine
Handwritten scrolls, dust-covered and old
Their hidden sagas silently unfold

Statues guard the silent lore
Their gazes locked on days of yore
Pages turning with a timeless grace
Histories we can scarcely trace

In the dark, the quiet reigns
Holding fast to ancient strains
Not lost, but hidden far from prime
Tales that drift through sands of time

Sheltered by Time's Veil

Veiled by the mists of long ago
Where gentle winds of ages blow
Sheltered truths bid time farewell
In the shadows, they safely dwell

The stars remember, the night does too
The secrets hiding from our view
Covered softly by the veil
Nurtured by the moonlight pale

In hidden realms, the past resides
Guarded where the quiet hides
Whispered secrets of ancient lore
Safely kept forever more

Veil of time, a gentle shroud
Encloses dreams, both faint and loud
Hidden safe within its fold
Stories waiting to be told

Hushed beneath the twilight's song
The echoes of old days belong
To the veil, where time gives grace
To mysteries lost in space

The Shrouded Chronicle

In the heart of twilight's gleam
Lie stories shrouded in dream
Quiet murmurs of what once was
Held in silence, just because

A shrouded chronicle unseen
Lies beneath time's serene
Guarding tales of joy and pain
Twined with fate's unwritten chain

In forgotten books and scrolls
Ancient fingers still unroll
Tales of kingdoms, myths untold
In the shrouded pages hold

Shadowed ink on parchment fades
In the cryptic, twilight glades
But the stories still remain
timeless in their secret reign

Time wraps them in a soft embrace
Leaves no hint, no single trace
Chronicles of days gone by
In the shrouds of ages lie

Cloak of the Elder Days

Draped in the cloak of elder days
Where history in silence plays
Legends whisper, stories wane
Through the mists of time they wane

Elders speak in tongues of old
Through this cloak, their tales unfold
Echoes of forgotten praise
In the heart of ancient maze

Cloaked in lore from yore's embrace
Whispers fill the empty space
Guardians of memories past
Timeless shadows they cast

Woven in the cloak's soft thread
Lost words linger, gently spread
Through the halls of endless time
In the echoes, they chime

Wrapped in fabric, old and worn
From the myths, new dreams are born
In the cloak, the past remains
Binding us in timeless chains

Forgotten Murmurs

In shadowed corners past the light,
Whispers float through silent air,
A language lost to creeping time,
Echoes of dreams that once lay bare.

The wind, it tells a sepia tale,
Of voices hushed, now ghostly veiled,
Each secret word wears dust anew,
Ineluctable as the morning dew.

A murmur here, a breathless sigh,
The remnants drift, they gently fly,
To realms where memories take flight,
Profound beneath the starry night.

Forgotten not by stones that stand,
But by the hearts in every land,
Yet sometimes, in the quiet woods,
We hear the murmurs' tender goods.

Ancient Refrains

Beyond the hills, where time lies still,
The echoes of old songs remain,
They hum through valleys, climb the crest,
And whisper down forgotten plains.

A melody of earth and sky,
Where ancient tales of life ensue,
Each note a thread, a woven tie,
Binding past to the present view.

The stars align with rhythmic grace,
And galaxies do softly hum,
The universe, in quiet space,
Resonates with a timeless drum.

In caves and stones, old lyrics sleep,
Awaiting breath to come alive,
A chorus of the past to keep,
Histories in each note revive.

Woven Memories

Threads of gold and strands of gray,
Woven through the fabric's hold,
Each stitch tells a story's sway,
Of warm embraces left untold.

Hands that crafted, hearts that beat,
In rhythms lost to time's cruel flow,
The tapestry, a living sheet,
Where old and new together grow.

In every thread, a memory lies,
A whispered word, a lover's vow,
Beneath the moon and sapphire skies,
The past and present here endow.

Through ages long and ages brief,
Made strong by hands, made soft by grief,
Woven memories intertwine,
Resilient through the fleeting line.

Fossils of Dreams

Beneath the earth's encasing hand,
Lie fossils of what dreams once spanned,
Each fragment holds a silent scream,
A relic of a bygone theme.

Encased in stone and hardened clay,
The dreams grow cold as ages sway,
Yet in their form, we see the light,
Of visions cast from endless night.

These remnants of the past endure,
A testament so pure, so sure,
In echoes of the dreams they were,
Fragile, yet they still allure.

We unearth them with care and grace,
Unveil the tale within their space,
Fossils of dreams, time can't erase,
Marking the passage of our race.

Ancient Whispers

Within the stones, old stories lie
Whispers of ages passing by
Silent guardians of lore stand tall
Echoes of life's primordial call

Underneath the forest's green cloak
Tales of the ancients softly spoke
In the rustle of leaves, truth's embrace
Wisdom hidden in nature's face

Layers of soil, secrets buried deep
In them, history's heartbeats sleep
From dawns of yore, whispers arise
Shadows of time under the skies

Waters flow and mountains erode
Stories traverse a timeless road
In fleeting whispers, legacies stay
Fading softly, then drift away

Listen closely, hear them speak clear
Voices of past, always near
Ancient whispers in the winds of time
Hushed verses in eternal rhyme

Beneath Time's Cloak

Behind the veil, where shadows play
Lies the past in an endless sway
Under the mantle of the years
Hidden truths, forgotten tears

With every moment, ages blend
Time's tapestry finds no end
Beneath its cloak, stories weave
Lives once lived, never to leave

Ancient paths, through time obscure
Footprints fade but memories endure
In each breath, whispers of old
Lives in fragments, tales retold

Silent nights, the stars ignite
Maps of history in their light
Beneath time's cloak, we all abide
In the ebb and flow, low and tide

From epochs past to future's dawn
In time's embrace, we're all drawn
Under its cloak, life and death conspire
In their dance, one heart's desire

Echoes of Antiquity

In ruins deep, the echoes call
From ancient halls where myths enthrall
Soft murmurs from the earth arise
From lands where time eternally lies

Granite bastions, silent and grand
Mute witnesses of an ancient land
Through wind and rain, they stand so tall
Echoes of past, they gently appall

In the dust of ages, stories reside
Echoes of souls, forever tied
In each fragment, a whisper clear
History's song only few can hear

Across the sands, through time they weave
Echoes the ancients left to conceive
In each grain, a tale to be told
Of courage, love, and kingdoms bold

Listen close to the silence speak
In every relic, a secret to seek
Echoes of antiquity softly hum
In the silent reverie, they become

Draped in Yesterday

In dreams of old, where shadows play
Lives and moments softly lay
Draped in yesterday, stories sleep
In heart and mind, forever keep

Through mist and twilight, echoes soar
Tales of yore on time's shore
In each whisper, a lesson lies
Where yesterday's spirit never dies

In ancient eyes, the past resides
Memories flow like gentle tides
Draped in yesterday's soft embrace
Time's touch, we all retrace

The winds of past through ages blow
Stories of life, love, and woe
Beneath the stars, under open sky
Yesterday's visions never die

Within us all, the past does speak
In silent moments, hearts it seeks
Draped in yesterday, we find our way
From dawn of past, to present day

Cloaks of Antiquity

In shadows deep, the echoes play,
Whispers of a time gone past,
Cloaks of antiquity, gently sway,
In the twilight, shadows last.

Across the pages, ink has bled,
Stories woven, threads so fine,
Histories whisper, softly tread,
Through the ages, tales entwine.

Artifacts of ancient lore,
Guardians of secrets old,
Silent sentinels, evermore,
Mysteries in their folds.

From stone to parchment, tales are spun,
In the dusk of old façade,
Timeless echoes, never done,
Guarded truths, they softly nod.

Beneath the twilight's gentle shroud,
Ancestral voices rise,
Cloaks of antiquity, so proud,
In history's embrace, we prize.

Subtle Embrace of the Past

In the quiet of the morn,
Memories softly creep,
Subtle whispers, gently born,
From the past, in dreams they seep.

Old roads lead to yesteryears,
In their winding, secrets hide,
Through the vale of time and tears,
Boundless tales, the paths provide.

Seasons change yet shadows stay,
Faint reminders, etched in gold,
In the heart where they replay,
Stories of the lives we hold.

Voices lost but not forgotten,
Echoes in the hall of time,
From foundations once begotten,
History's cryptic rhyme.

In the dusk, a gentle sigh,
Subtle as the evening mist,
Through the past, our spirits fly,
By the bygone, gently kissed.

Mist-Wrapped Chronicles

Through the forest, mist-wrapped green,
Ancient tales, the whispers tell,
Of the years that lie between,
In the silence, legends dwell.

Mist-enshrouded, pathways fade,
Memories ghostlike in the air,
Chronicles through time conveyed,
Invisible yet everywhere.

Voices murmur through the lea,
Shadowed chronicles unfold,
In the hush of reverie,
In the mist, the past is told.

Gently veiled in twilight's sheen,
History's ghostly tendrils wind,
Through the valleys, evergreen,
Stories of another kind.

Ancient echoes of the world,
Mist-wrapped chronicles, still bright,
In the folds, the past unfurled,
Whispers through the soft twilight.

Curtain Calls of History

When the final act is near,
Curtains slowly start to fall,
Ancient voices reappear,
Echoes through the ages call.

Stage of time, where shadows play,
Scenes of yore in silence bloom,
Through the ages, day by day,
History in twilight's gloom.

Hidden scripts of long-lost days,
Written in the sands of time,
Ancient actors in their ways,
Dance upon the aged rhyme.

In the quiet, twilight deep,
Curtains parting, past unfolds,
Ancient secrets softly weep,
In the dusk, the story holds.

Whispers in the final light,
Curtain calls of history,
In the fading, gentle night,
Past's embrace, eternally.

Mists of the Forgotten

In shadows where the echoes dwell,
The secrets of the past do swell,
Veiled beneath an ancient spell,
In mists the whispers softly tell.

A time of lore, a world unseen,
Where dreams and memories convene,
Amid the silence, twilight sheen,
The realm of what has never been.

Through foggy veils, the specters sigh,
The echoes of the days gone by,
Lost tales beneath the starry sky,
In mists they live, they never die.

A world erased, now barely known,
In silvered mists, the seeds are sown,
Of stories lost, of spirits grown,
They dance in twilight, they're alone.

In shadows where the past does fade,
In mists of time, the dreams are made,
A place where light and dark invade,
Existence in a ghostly shade.

Beneath Time's Whisper

In silent tones, the ages speak,
Through whispers soft, through voices weak,
In layers deep, through time we seek,
The echoes faint and mystique.

From ancient dawns to twilight's end,
Where past and present slowly blend,
Through eras gone around the bend,
Time's whispers gently condescend.

Beneath the flow of temporal streams,
Are woven threads of unknown dreams,
In ceaseless dance, time's silent schemes,
Of whispers soft in muted themes.

In quiet nights where shadows brood,
Amidst the still and poignant mood,
The whisperings of time intrude,
On hearts laid bare and dreams pursued.

Eternal tales, forever spun,
Between the stars, beneath the sun,
In whispers where the ages run,
Time speaks in silence to each one.

Under the Ancestral Shroud

Beneath the earth, where secrets sleep,
In silent tombs, in caverns deep,
The echoes of the past we keep,
In shadowed halls where ancestors weep.

Through winding paths of memory,
In whispered tales and history,
The shroud reveals the legacy,
Of lives obscured in mystery.

Through time's embrace, the visions fade,
Of lives once lived and debts once paid,
In sacred ground, in silent shade,
Their stories wait in solemn staid.

The shroud that wraps the ancient night,
Conceals the past from mortal sight,
Yet in its folds, the spirits light,
A flame that burns through endless flight.

Beneath the canopy of time,
In shrouded depths, the past does rhyme,
Ancestral songs in hushed mime,
Await the key in silent prime.

Enwrapped in History's Lament

In twilight hues, the echoes wail,
Of times long past, of sorrow's tale,
Within the folds where shadows trail,
We linger hearing history's hail.

Enwrapped in folds of distant days,
In mournful tones and silvered grays,
Where ancient songs in sorrow plays,
The voices of the past convey.

The pages turned in silent night,
In whispered lore, in fading light,
The stories drift beyond our sight,
Of history's lamenting plight.

Through broken dreams and withered art,
In silent grief, the voices part,
Their mournful song, a somber heart,
Of pasts enwrapped in silent start.

In twilight's dusk, where time suspends,
The echoes of the past ascend,
To futures where the tales blend,
In history's lament, we comprehend.

Draped in Silent Silence

The night descends, a curtain drawn
Upon a world of quiet peace
Where whispers, once in daylight shone
Now softly fade, their echoes cease

Stars above, in mute array
Gaze down with silent, solemn grace
They tell of worlds far, far away
In silence, vast expanses trace

The moonlight drapes the earth in white
A satin veil of softest hue
Each shadow, wrapped in gentle night
In silence, finds its own debut

No wind to rustle sleeping leaves
No owl or creature's distant call
In perfect stillness, time deceives
The silent world, entranced by all

In silence, every heartbeats clear
A symphony, no sound can sway
As night holds all that we hold dear
In silence, till the break of day

Muffled Voices of the Past

Through cobblestone and weathered street
The whispers travel, soft and fast
They tell of lives that once did meet
In muffled voices of the past

The echoes of a yesteryear
Where laughter rang and hearts were strong
Now linger like a fleeting tear
A distant, melancholic song

Beneath the archways, shadows play
Their silent dance, a solemn cast
As time, relentless, seeks to fray
The muffled voices of the past

Old windows gaze with hollow eyes
On scenes they witnessed, long gone by
They hold the secrets, hushed and wise
Of loves and losses, whispered sighs

Yet in the murmur of the breeze
The past persists, forever fast
In quiet tones it brings to ease
The muffled voices of the past

Forgotten by the Seasons

In autumn's glow, the leaves descend
A tapestry of gold and red
Where summer dreams and winter send
Their whispers, of a time now fled

The springtime blooms that once did blaze
With vibrant hues and sweet perfume
Are but a distant, fading phase
Forgotten by the seasons' loom

The winter's chill, with icy hand
Erases all that once was green
And summer's warmth, by time is spanned
As seasons shift, an unseen scene

Each cycle brings a new refrain
While old ones fade to memory
The seasons turn, and yet remain
A fleeting, endless reverie

Forgotten dreams in nature's scroll
Of spring, and summer, autumn's wane
The seasons take and then unroll
Their tale, again, in endless chain

Veiled in Memory's Fog

Through mists of time, the past is veiled
Its clear lines blurred by memory's hand
Fragmented scenes, where truth has failed
Beneath the fog, where shadows stand

Once vivid moments, sharp and bright
Now softened by the touch of years
In memory's fog, both day and night
Are woven with forgotten tears

The faces, places, once held clear
Blend softly in a gauzy screen
Yet through the haze, some echoes steer
A haunting, almost seen, unseen

In dreams they walk, the long-lost days
And whisper tales, both sweet and sad
Their voices lost in memory's haze
Yet somehow, still, make heartbeats glad

Though memory's fog may shroud and hide
The essence of what once was known
These ghostly echoes, by our side
In veiled remembrance, we have grown

Yesteryear Echoes

Whispers on the silent breeze
Tales of times we used to roam
Memories of distant seas
Echo softly, call us home

Beneath the stars, our spirits play
Waltzing through the twilight haze
Moments lost to dawn's first ray
Lingering in a golden daze

Laughter carried through the night
Fading as the shadows grow
In the stillness, pure delight
From yesteryear in ebb and flow

Old guitars in twilight strum
Songs that fade like morning dew
From past days, those tunes still hum
Whispering secrets old and true

Faces framed in sepia tones
Alive within our hearts' embrace
Yesteryear's echoes, quiet moans
In time's reflection, pure grace

Winds from the Past

Softly through the pines they weave
Tales of love and battles won
Ancient echos we perceive
Kissed by moon, warmed by sun

Silent whispers through the trees
Legends of the days gone by
Carrying tales on midnight breeze
Of days we lived, of times we cried

Winds from yonder, east and west
Bring with them the songs long gone
In their murmur, soothe and rest
Memories that linger on

Ancient whispers fill the air
Lifted on the wings of time
Carrying past dreams we share
In the winds' enchanted rhyme

Serenade in twilight's glow
Moments laced in time's embrace
Winds from past, they gently blow
Bringing peace, a soft solace

Curtains of Time

Drawn between the night and day
Veil of moments we have known
Shadows dance, then fade away
In the silence, seeds are sown

Curtains lifting, stories told
Ghostly whispers, pure and fine
Secrets ventured, hearts unfold
Through the parted veil of time

In the folds, a tale revealed
Ancient whispers, hidden lore
Each a secret long concealed
Held within the twilight's door

Curtains part, the echoes sing
Of the past and future hence
Woven into everything
Mingling in the present tense

Faintly through the mists they glide
Specters of both joy and strife
Curtains part, and there inside
Lies the essence of our life

Ghosts of Forgotten Days

Shadows long since gone astray
Wander through our dreams unceased
Whispering of yesterday
Echoes of the past released

Faint and fleeting, pale they roam
Ghosts of days we left behind
In the twilight's shaded dome
Lost in corridors of mind

Memories in muted hues
Flicker like a candle's flame
Moments we can never lose
Though their substance brings no name

Specters in the dusky light
Fade into the shades of grey
Haunting us in silent night
From the ghosts of yesterday

Eternal footprints on the sands
Traces of a time long past
Gently held in fragile hands
Ghostly echoes, shadows cast

Milton Keynes UK
Ingram Content Group UK Ltd.
UKHW011608130624
443933UK00004B/71